A HANDFUL OF ADVENT:

Preaching and Worship Resources for Year B

Delmer Chilton

and John Fairless

DEDICATION

Because Advent is where we begin, again.

CONTENTS

ACKNOWLEDGMENTS

Scripture versions quoted here are from the New Revised Standard Version.

Watch for the Light, c. Plough Publishing House, 2001

Most of the rest of the work is original – we think.

Delmer Chilton with John Fairless

Every year we celebrate the holy season of Advent, O God. Every year we pray those beautiful prayers of longing and waiting, and sing those lovely songs of hope and promise. Every year we roll up all our needs and yearnings and faithful expectation into one word: "Come!"

And yet, what a strange prayer this is! After all, you have already come and pitched your tent among us. You have already shared our life with its little joys, its long days of tedious routine, its bitter end. Could we invite you to anything more than this with our "Come"? Could you approach any nearer to us than you did when you became the "Son of Man"? In spite of all this we still pray: "Come."

-- Karl Rahner, in *Watch for the Light*

(used by permission)

Delmer Chilton with John Fairless

AND SO, IT BEGINS (WHAT IS THIS BOOK ABOUT?)

Who doesn't love Advent?

Depending on your tradition and personal (pastoral) practice, Advent may symbolize the real "start" of the holiday season – or, at least, it is an extended time of preparation and anticipation for the joy of Christmas. Of course, for many pastors and church staff members, Advent typically coincides with a very busy calendar of service and social obligations, too, so the joy is often tempered by a fair amount of stress!

As working pastors with more than a few Advent/Christmas seasons between us, we thought it might be helpful to write this book to help ease some of the stress of the season. As with all of our thoughts, we are certainly not trying to say that we have found THE WAY to work and worship through Advent; there simply is no THE WAY to do things in the Church, no matter which part of it you serve.

What we offer here are some ideas, plans, resources (including sermons, of course) and just general observations that we have found helpful. Maybe you will, as well.

The book is laid out to proceed from the earliest stages of planning your Advent calendar, and proceeds with a number of (we hope) helpful resources such as Advent devotionals, calls to worship, litanies of praise, and other needful folderol, thus proceeding to the heart of the work: texts, comments, and a sermon for each of the four Sundays in Advent. There are additional services (such as the *Hanging of the Greens* and a *Service of Lessons and Carols*,) and some hymn and musical suggestions, as well.

The writing, as usual with *Two Bubbas and a Bible*, is intermingled between Delmer and John. As Delmer is fond of saying, "We are one person with two heads" when we write and teach. Sermons and special services are the province of Delmer; supporting materials and comments are mostly by John.

Why is this **"A Handful of Advent?"** If you have been around us much, you have mostly likely heard Delmer's seminal preaching story about the wonderful use of the texts from Isaiah. If you haven't, we promise we'll tell it for you the first opportunity we get. Meanwhile, dig in…and enjoy!

Christ is coming!

A HANDFUL OF ADVENT

THINGS TO DECIDE AS SOON AS POSSIBLE

Advent is a short and somewhat hurried season, with lots of things going on outside the church competing for time with things on the church calendar. It is important to make some choices early so that the church staff can plan services and get the word out to the congregation so that they, in turn, can plan their holiday activities with an eye on the church calendar. This is an annotated check-list to help you with your planning.

1) Choir "Cantata" – if, and when –

For some congregations, this a no-brainer – "We've always done it, we've always done it on the third Sunday of Advent, we still have an adequate choir to do it well." For others, not so much. Some have never done it and should think about doing it. Others have been doing it for a long time and can no longer do it well and should consider not doing it.

As to timing – if Christmas Day is a Monday, that means Christmas Eve services will be on the evening of the Fourth Sunday of Advent. This might be a good Sunday to have a Cantata or an Advent Service of Lessons and Carols (see p.) in the morning, and your congregations traditional Christmas Eve service(s) in the evening. Also, the Third Sunday in Advent has been a popular time for cantatas because it has, in many liturgical denominations, been known as "Gaudete" Sunday, after the first word in the once standard Epistle for this day, Philippians 4:4 "Rejoice in the Lord always . . ." As Gaudete, or Rejoice Sunday, it signals a shift to a lighter tome and was once marked with the pink candle in the Advent Wreath.

2) Special Devotional Services in Advent?

In connection with its beginnings as "Little," or "Saint Martin's" Advent, some congregations hold extra mid-week services in Advent. As with the Choir Cantata, if your congregation has been doing these, should the tradition be continued? If they have not, would it be well to start? When would the services be held? Would there be a meal or fellowship time before or after the services? What liturgy would be used? Would there be a sermon or "devotion?" What is the unifying theme or subject of the devotions?

3) What is your "Narrative Arc" for the four Sundays of Advent?

Working with the Revised Common Lectionary texts for the season and the themes laid out in the following section, "**The Narrative Arc,**" congregation worship leaders need to be clear about what part of the story they are working with on each Sunday. This facilitates hymn selection, choir or special music choices and the writing of the Prayers of the People.

4) The Advent Wreath

This has become so popular that almost all Catholic and mainline Protestant parishes have an Advent wreath. Some of the questions to consider are placement, color of candles, when in the service will it be lighted, devotions to be read or prayed, who does the lighting and the devotions. In most congregations, some of this is established by tradition but the pastor and/or worship team have responsibility for picking the actual devotions, hymns or songs used, etc.

(See p. 21 for Advent Devotion help.)

5) When (and how) to decorate?

Again, some of this is dictated by denominational and congregational tradition, but there is some leeway and choices need to be made on many timing and taste questions. How soon do we put up a tree in the worship space? Will it be a "Christmas," or a "Chrismon" tree? When do we "hang the greens?" i.e. put up other decorations? How long do they stay up?

6) When can we sing Christmas carols?

This is a major bone of contention in some Lutheran and Episcopal parishes, particularly ones with a significant number of people who are converts from more "free church," non-liturgical denominations. The standard teaching in this regard is that Christmas carols should not be sung until Christmas, which begins in the evening on Christmas Eve. This presents an interesting and somewhat confusing problem for people accustomed from their youth to singing them in church all through December and hearing them on TV, Radio, and shopping malls all the time after Halloween. As a Lutheran pastor who has also served an Episcopal parish, Delmer developed a strategy of creating many opportunities for singing Christmas carols in December, at times other than Sunday morning worship: Children's Christmas program, going out caroling, as part of an evening Choir Cantata, etc. Also, *"Joy to the World"* is listed in the *Evangelical Lutheran Worship* Hymnal as an Advent hymn, so he used that on the Third of fourth Sunday of Advent.

For both items 5 and 6, education and compromise, and a constant awareness among the worship leaders that worship has two purposes: to glorify God and to edify the congregation. Bluntly put, if the congregation is sitting there angry and confused – not a lot of glorifying or edifying is going on.

THE NARRATIVE ARC OF ADVENT

Yogi Berra famously said, "If you don't know where you're going you might end us someplace else." This is particularly true of preaching in Advent. There are many narratives and stories competing for the church's attention in the time between **Christ the King** and **The Nativity of Our Lord,** i.e. "Thanksgiving 'til Christmas." It's hard for the preacher to know where to point the attention of her listeners, how to bring focus to the congregation's observance of Advent.

For most folks, including most of our church members, December is a time to plan for a family celebration that has vaguely religious overtones. Most of the message the culture portrays is one of sentimental (and material) concern for loved ones, plus occasional forays into an extra effort to helping the less fortunate. The Biblical "Christmas Story," is mined for images to reinforce this vision: the "Holy Family," the generosity of the innkeeper, the gifts brought by the Magi; mixed in bits from the secular Christmas stories of Santa Claus, Ebenezer Scrooge, the Little Drummer Boy, the Grinch, etc. etc.

The texts selected for most of Advent are basically ignorant of this vision, and oftentimes work directly against it. For example, the First Reading on the First Sunday of Advent contains this line, *"We have all become like one who is unclean, and all our righteous deeds are like a filthy cloth. We all fade like a leaf, and our iniquities, like the wind, take us away."* (Isaiah 64:7)

Things don't get much better with the Gospel Lesson; it's the conclusion to Mark's version of Jesus' apocalyptic predictions: *"But in those days, after that suffering, the sun will be darkened, and the moon will not give its light . . ."* (Mark: 13:24)

This theme continues. On the Second Sunday: *"But the day of the Lord will come like a thief, and then the heavens will pass away with a loud noise, and the elements will be dissolved with fire, and the earth and everything that is done on it will be disclosed." (2* Peter 3:10) The Third Sunday starts off promisingly, but buried within words about Good News to the oppressed, binding up the brokenhearted, and proclaiming liberty to the captives, we hear these jarring words in the First Reading: *"the day of vengeance of our God,"* (Isaiah 61:2) which are followed by these words in the Magnificat, from the mouth of Jesus' sweet little Mama, *"He has scattered the proud. . . he has brought down the powerful from their thrones. . . and sent the rich away empty."* (from Luke 1:51-53) And speaking of Mary – the whole got engaged, got pregnant, her boyfriend's not the father, an angel told me it's God's baby, sent off to live with a distant relative so the village won't see her "baby bump," giving birth in a stable, or a spare room, or something like that – it's not really a Hallmark, family-friendly, Lifetime movie sort of story, is it? What is going on here?

The season of Advent has its roots in what is now southeast France and northeast Spain. In almost all early Christianity, Easter was the time for adult converts to be baptized and join the church. In this region France and Spain, Epiphany was also a popular time for baptisms.

The period of catechism and spiritual preparation for baptism before Easter evolved into Lent. In a similar fashion, the time of instruction and preparation before Epiphany was marked out as a season of fasting and prayer, with lengths varying over the years from forty days to six weeks. (*The Study of Liturgy*, Oxford, 1978, p. 416; *The Christian Liturgy*, Fortress Press,1997, Frank Senn, p. 161, p.190) Because the fifth century bishop of Tours declared that the laypeople should fast three days a week from the feast day of Saint Martin of Tours (Nov. 11) until the Epiphany, this six-week period became known as "St. Martin's Lent." In the late sixth century, Saint Gregory the Great refers to the "four weeks of Advent," in several of his sermons.

From the very beginning it has been difficult to decide if Advent is a time for penitence or hope, or both. This tension is revealed not only in the lectionary's choice of texts, but also in the liturgical churches tradition of not singing Christmas carols until Christmas Eve. Meanwhile, the world gets started making merry and singing Christmas songs, sometimes before Thanksgiving. Within the liturgical traditions this tension is revealed in more subtle ways: the shift in recent years from Lenten penitential purple (traditional in Catholicism, Anglicanism, Lutheranism, and other Protestants who use vestments) to a more cheerful and hopeful blue (traditional among the Swedes and in the Sarum Rite) as the color of paraments, vestments and candles; the traditional celebration of the Third Sunday as Gaudete, "Rejoice" Sunday after the first word of the traditional lectionary's Second Lesson – Philippians 4:4 "Rejoice in the Lord always, again I will say rejoice."

In *Christian Liturgy (p. 190),* Frank Senn says that a survey of lectionary schemes from the 9th through the 12th centuries show 10 standard Gospel lessons for Advent, gathered around four basic themes:

   1) – The end of the world and the signs of the times

      Luke 21:25ff.; Matthew 24:37-44; Matthew 25:1-13

   2) –The triumphal entry of Christ into Jerusalem

      Matthew 21:1-9

   3) – The mission of John the Baptist

      John 1:9ff.; Luke 1:3ff.; Mark 1:1-8; Matthew 11:2ff

   4) - The Annunciation and Visitation

      Luke 1:26-38; 1:39-56 (with *Magnificat*)

The Revised Common Lectionary continues to reflect this basic outline, with the texts for the four Sundays clustering around similar ideas:

First Sunday: The "Day of the Lord" and the signs of the times

Second Sunday: The Promise of a Messiah

Third Sunday: John the Baptist points out the Messiah

Fourth Sunday: Mary and Joseph and a surprising pregnancy

Bernard of Clairvaux helpfully stated the overall message of Advent as "The Coming of Christ," and further clarified that in this liturgical season we are:

1) **Remembering** that Christ came **in the flesh** at Bethlehem,
2) **Preparing** for Christ to come daily **in our community** and **in our hearts**
3) **Anticipating** Christ coming again **in the Second Coming.**

Preaching in Advent is a matter of weaving the texts and themes together to present a coherent and compelling message about being prepared for Christ to come in our lives, in our church, and in our world. In year B, this might look something like this.

The First Sunday: The First and Second comings are tied together by partnering the little apocalypse from Mark's gospel (13:24-37), the reproach and call to repentance in Isaiah 64, with a reference in 1 Corinthians to being "blameless on the day of the Lord Jesus." The sermon on the day could focus on the why of Christ's coming; our sin and the hope God's forgiveness, our need and the assurance of God's provision; our loneliness and God's promise to be present with us. Some mention could be made of the ways one can go about getting ready for "the Day of the Lord:" repentance, prayer, fasting, and acts of charity in the world. This is the primary "little Lent," day of the modern Advent.

The Second Sunday: On this day, John the Baptist is paired with Isaiah 40 as the voice crying out to prepare the way of the Lord. This main theme is bolstered by 2 Peter's apocalyptic vision and promise of salvation on the "day of God." Preaching on this day could focus on maintaining awareness and hope that because God came to us in the past, we can be certain that God in Christ will continue to be present with us now and in the future.

The Third Sunday: Today we again focus on John the Baptist, but in our reading from John's gospel, the focus is on the Baptist's role in pointing to Jesus as the Christ as an example that we, as individuals and as the church, are invited to follow. Our call is to be busy being a part of God's loving actions in the world while also pointing people to God's love shown for them in Christ's life, death and resurrection.

The Fourth Sunday: Today, we have the first explicit reference in the Lectionary texts to what most people think of as the Christmas Story. (Although on the Third Sunday, the Magnificat [Luke 1:46b-55] is listed as an alternate to the appointed Psalm.) 2 Samuel uses a play on words; i.e. *house* as *temple* (7:5,6) and *house* as *dynasty* or *family lineage (7:15-16,* to present the promise of God that the legitimate king of Israel will always be a descendant of David. This promise is remembered in Luke 1:27, 32-33. Of course, the primary focus of the Gospel text is the conversation between the angel Gabriel and the virgin Mary. Here the three emphases mentioned by Bernard are brought tightly together. Joseph, House of David, Mary, *"bear a Son,"* cause us to explicitly **remember** that Christ came to us in Bethlehem, 2000 years ago. Mary's confusion about, and then acceptance of her role, call us to **prepare** ourselves and our community for Christ to come. **Anticipating** the Second Coming is not explicit in the text, but it is implied in 1:33b – "**... of his kingdom there will be no end.**"

THE HANGING OF THE GREENS

(Some Christian communities decorate the worship space for Advent and Christmas on or before the First Sunday in Advent. Others delay Christmas decorations until later in December. This devotional service is designed to flexible and adaptable to local needs and traditions.)

GATHERING

Gathering Song   <u>Prepare the Royal Highway</u>

Call to Worship and Prayer of the Day

Leader: How dear to me is your dwelling, O Lord of Hosts!

People: Happy are they who dwell in your house!

   They will always be praising you! (Psalm 84: 1, 4)

Leader: I was glad when they said to me –

People: Let us go to the house of the Lord. (Psalm 122:1)

Leader: Let us pray together

People: O God of great surprises, we come today to prepare your house, and our hearts, to receive you.

Bless the adornments with which we decorate this holy space.

May each thing we place around this room remind us of your grace, love, and presence with us —

not only here but everywhere.

In the name of the One Who Comes we pray. AMEN.

WORD

First   Reading: Exodus 35:21-29

Second   Reading: Mark 13:33-37

A brief meditation on outward and inward preparation to receive Christ may follow.

Those responsible (Altar Guild, Worship Committee, etc.) take over at this point and direct the Hanging of the Greens. When the work is done, the community will regather.

REFLECTIONS AND PRAYERS

Re-Gathering   Song   <u>Rejoice, Rejoice Believers</u>

A Litany of Blessing

Leader: We have placed Advent wreaths upon our doors.

People: To invite and welcome all people to wait with us for the Lord.

Leader: We have placed bright candles in our window sills.

People: To invite and welcome the bright light of God's Word into our lives.

Leader: We have hung green garlands around the room.

People: To invite and welcome the gift of eternal life into our midst.

Leader: We have set up and decorated a Christmon tree.

People: To invite and welcome the One who fulfills all God's promises.

Leader: We have set out a creche - with Mary and Joseph, animals and shepherds.

People: To invite and welcome our adoration and praise of the Incarnate One.

Leader: We have left the manger empty.

People: To invite and welcome the Christ Child into our hearts

Leader: I invite any of you who wish to share any thoughts, experiences, or insights from our work together today.

(Please limit yourself to 2-3 minutes.)

Closing Prayer. Blessing, Dismissal

Leader: Let us pray together

People: O God of Past, Present and Future,

bless the work that we have done this day,

be with us now as we impatiently await your promised Messiah,

fill all our days with hope,

and give us faith that you will come and save. AMEN

Leader: May God bless you and keep you.

May God's face shine on you and be gracious to you.

May God look upon you with favor + and give you peace.

People: **AMEN**

Leader: The Lord is coming! Alleluia!

People: **The Lord is coming indeed! Alleluia!**

Delmer Chilton with John Fairless

RITES OF PREPARATION

Confession and Forgiveness for Advent – B

(Based on 1 John 1:8-9, Isaiah 64:1-9, Isaiah 40:1-11, Isaiah 61:1-4; 2 Corinthians 13:13)

Minister: We gather in the Name of the Holy Trinity –

the Creator who made us,

the Incarnate One + who redeems us,
the Holy Spirit who fills our lives with light and love.

People: AMEN.

Minister: If we claim, "We don't have any sin," we deceive ourselves and the truth is not in us. But if we confess our sins, God is faithful and just, and will forgive our sins and cleanse us from everything we've done wrong." Let us come before God with open hearts and contrite spirits –

People: We have become unclean;

All our attempts at goodness fail.
We fade like a leaf,
and our sins, like the wind, take us away
away from you, O Lord,
and away from our true selves.

But now we hear the voice of one crying in the wilderness

and we yearn to change our ways,

to turn from evil in the direction of your goodness.

We confess to you, O Lord,

that our ways are not straight,

that we are lost in a wilderness of our own making,

we cannot find our way out.

But we vaguely remember, O Lord,

that you have sent the Anointed One into our lives

to bring us Good News.

We plead this day,

that your Son will once again,

bind up our broken hearts,

liberate us from our captivity to sin,

release us from the prison-house of our desires

and restore us to your loving presence.

O Lord, do not remember our iniquity forever. Amen

Minister   Hear these words of grace and forgiveness from the Holy Scriptures: "Comfort, O Comfort my people," says your God, "Speak tenderly, and cry to them that . . . their penalty is paid."   As a minister of the church of Jesus Christ, and in obedience to his command, I declare to you this eternal truth - yours sins are forgiven by the grace of our Lord Jesus Christ + and the love of God; therefore, you now live each day in the loving communion of the Holy Spirit. **AMEN**

ADVENT WREATH DEVOTIONS

1) Use the Hymn *"Light One Candle to Watch for Messiah"*
   The Hymn has four verses, each one keyed to the Sunday in Advent.
   i.e. verse 1 starts, *"Light one candles,"* verse 2 - *"Light two candles,"* etc.

Here's how the themes match up with the texts:

Advent 1 –

Verse one – *"He shall bring salvation to Israel, God fulfills the promise"*

Lesson – Psalm 80:2 - *Stir up your might and come and save us.*

Advent 2 –

Verse 2 – *He shall feed the flock like a shepherd, gently lead them homeward*

Lesson – Isaiah 40:11 – *He will feed his flock like a shepherd,*

he will carry the lambs in his arms,

and carry them in his bosom,

and gently lead the mother sheep.

Advent 3 –

Verse 3 – *"Lift your heads and lift high the gateway for the king of glory."*

Lesson – Psalm 126: 1-2a – *When the Lord restored the fortunes of Zion*

we were like those who dream.

Then our mouth filled with laughter,

and our tongue with shouts of joy.

Advent 4 –

Verse 4 – *"He is coming, tell the glad tidings, Let your lights be shining."*

Lesson – Luke 1:32 *"He will be great, and will be called the Son of the Most High, And the Lord God will give him the throne of his ancestor David."*

"Light One Candle to Watch for Messiah" can be found in several hymnals, including:

Evangelical Lutheran Church in America

- *With One Voice* – Augsburg Fortress, 1995 and

- *Evangelical Lutheran Worship* – Augsburg Fortress, 2006

The Presbyterian Church – USA

-- *Glory to God – The Presbyterian Hymnal* - PC(USA), 2013

THE DEVOTIONS

(Each Sunday, the appropriate verse of the hymn "Light One Candle" is sung as the correct candle on the Advent wreath is lit.)

The First Sunday in Advent –

Leader: In Psalm 80:2 we read - *"Stir up your might and come and save us."*

Advent is a time of waiting, but it is not a time of passivity, not a time of impatiently sitting around until the baby Jesus and Sant Claus show up on Christmas Day. Advent invites us to be busy – not only with decorating, and buying presents, and planning visits with friends and loved ones – but also with personal prayer and self-reflection, with acts of love and generosity to friends and strangers, and with attendance at worship in the community of faith. God has promised to Come. We are invited to get ready.

Let us pray.

People: O Lord, with the Psalmist we cry out to you and implore you to come.

"Stir up your might and come and save us." Turn our hearts away from ourselves and toward our neighbor. As we wait for you to come and save us, teach us to go and busy ourselves helping and saving others. Amen.

The Second Sunday in Advent

Leader: Isaiah 40:11– the prophet says

> " *He will feed his flock like a shepherd, he will carry the lambs in his arms, and carry them in his bosom, and gently lead the mother sheep.* "

The shepherd is one of the more enduring images of the Bible. David was a shepherd before he was made king. The kings of Israel were often said to be the shepherd of the people. When the prophets complained about a bad king, they frequently called him a bad shepherd who had failed to take care of his flock. Even if we know very little of the Bible by heart, most of us can recite the 23rd Psalm, which begins, "The Lord is my shepherd." When Isaiah wanted to reassure the Isreali people in exile that the Lord their God had not forgotten them, he drew word pictures of a good shepherd, feeding, carrying, leading the people. The coming, the "advent," of the Messiah, the Good Shepherd is near. Let us pray.

People: O Lord, come to us like a shepherd. We, like sheep, have often gone astray. We are much distracted by the world around us. Help us to listen for your voice, and to follow where you lead. Come to us where we are and bring us home. Amen.

The Third Sunday in Advent

Leader: Psalm 126:1-2a says -

When the Lord restored the fortunes of Zion we were like those who dream. Then our mouth filled with laughter, and our tongue with shouts of joy.

We have all gone through tough times; periods when we feel like our string of bad luck will never end, when "fortune" has indeed turned her fickle back upon us. Israel often went through such hard times, and because they were aware of being the "chosen people," they experienced the added pain of thinking they had done something wrong and were being punished, or that God had turned away and forgotten them. No wonder they were "like those who go out weeping, carrying the seed." But the Psalmist reminded them of the good news of God's grace, ". . .the Lord restored the fortunes of Zion."

That promise comes to us as well. We await the coming of the Lord who will restore our fortunes, who will do great things for us. Let us pray

People: O King of Glory - as you draw near, we lift our heads, our hearts, and our voices.

We hear the call of the one crying in the wilderness; we know you are close by. Come to us - dry our tears, straighten our backs, elevate our spirits. Fill our hearts with happiness and our hearts with laughter. Send us out to spread the Good News, "The night of mourning is almost over, the dawn of joy is near." Amen.

The Fourth Sunday in Advent

Leader: In Luke's Gospel, The angel Gabriel tells Mary about her unborn child:

"He will be great, and will be called the Son of the Most High,

And the Lord God will give him the throne of his ancestor David." Luke 1:32

"They went to Bethlehem . . . because Joseph was of the house and lineage of David."

When this line is read on Christmas Eve, our minds often run right past it to get to the good part; the pregnant mother on a donkey, the worried father, the unwritten about innkeeper, the shepherds, the angels, the animals (who aren't mentioned either.). Except as an explanation of why Jesus was born in

Bethlehem, this lineage business doesn't seem to matter. But it does, it really does. In Samuel, God promises David that ". . . the Lord will make you a house." He means a kingly line that will last forever. The Jewish people believed that the coming Messiah would be a descendant of David. As Gabriel said – "the Lord will give him the throne of David." With his death and resurrection, Jesus transformed this kingship into an agency of peace, not of power. We are invited today to welcome the Son of David, the Prince of Peace - into our world, into our homes, and into our hearts. Let us pray:

People: O One Who Comes – we yearn for your arrival in our midst. We long for you to come and fill our hearts with your love and our lives with your light. We eagerly await your advent here. Come and stay with us, and teach us the ways of peace. AMEN.

CALLS TO WORSHIP

First Sunday in Advent (Based on Isaiah 64:1-9)

O, Lord – come down!

Come down in the midst of our chaos and confusion, come down into our all-too-busy lives; come down, Lord, into hearts that desire to open up to you. We need you to come down – though we tremble at the prospect!

We have heard the stories of days past – when your presence caused mountains to quake and nations to tremble.

We have heard how the heavens were torn apart, and how you did awesome deeds!

We admit that most of our trembling is from fear, not of you, but of the powers that haunt and hinder us. We have felt far from you, God, as if you had hidden your face and turned away from us.

Do not be angry with us any longer; your love, like that of a father – your tenderness, like that of a mother – Lord, that is what we seek.

Come down, come down, come visit and console us!

Come down, O Lord, and live among us; we are your people and we praise you!

Amen.

Second Sunday in Advent (Based on Mark 1:1-8)

It's only the beginning, people of God!

All that God has done and will do – from the ancient words of Isaiah to the pronouncement of John the Baptizer – it's only the beginning of the wonder of Christ.

We are called to prepare the way – we are getting ready for God's path-straightening, valley-lifting work among us!

In the wilderness places and at the rivers of our lives, let us raise our voices in worship and praise.

Come, let us worship; come, Holy Spirit.

Begin anew in us the life of Jesus Christ!

Amen.

Third Sunday in Advent (Based on Psalm 126)

Is it a dream, Lord? Could it possibly be true?

Our lives are filled with tears in this season; and yet, you have promised shouts of joy.

We remember the days when you did great things for us – we remember, and we rejoice.

This day, great God, our hope for the future – this day, let the waters of praise flow forth.

May the seeds of faith we sow here this day spring forth into sheaves of abundance and blessing.

May it be so – Amen!

Fourth Sunday in Advent (based on Romans 16:25-27)

God, you are our Strength!

Lord, you are our Wisdom.

You are worthy of glory forever, Eternal One, for you are revealing to the world the One who has come to save us from our sins.

We worship You as we proclaim Jesus Christ this day.

Accept our praise and our obedience – and strengthen us to welcome your Son, our Savior.

Amen and amen!

EUCHARISTIC PRAYER FOR ADVENT

Dialog

    Minister: The Lord be with you.

    People: And also with you.

    Minister: Lift up your hearts.

    People: We lift them up to the Lord.

    Minister: Let us give thanks to the Lord our God.

    People: It is right to give God our thanks and praise.

Preface

    Minister: It is a good, right, and joyful thing that we should,

        at all times and in all places,

        give thanks and praise to you, O God,

        our creator and sustainer.

        Through prophets and preachers,

        patriarchs and matriarchs,

        kings and queens,

        those in high places

        and those who simply tilled the soil,

        harvested the grain,

        made the wine,

        or tended the sheep

        - you have reached out to us in word and deed

        to teach, guide, rebuke and inspire us.

        And then you sent to us the greatest gift of all,

        the gift of yourself

in the person of your Son,

Jesus Christ our Lord.

And so, with Mary and Joseph,

Elizabeth and Zechariah,

all the saints above

and all the sinners below,

we unite our voices in heaven's eternal song

of thanksgiving and praise:

Holy, Holy, Holy, Lord,

God of power and might.

Heaven and earth are full of your glory.

Hosanna in the highest.

Blessed is the one who comes in the name of the Lord.

Hosanna in the highest.

Eucharistic Prayer

Blessed are you,

O Lord of the universe and Lord of our hearts,

we praise you for

your power and your tenderness;

your justice and your mercy,

your demand that we be righteous

and your command that we love one another.

On this day,

we have recall the many times

you have rescued your people from themselves

and have promised to lift us up and revive us, again.

On this day,

we celebrate the promise fulfilled

in Jesus of Nazareth,

Jesus, the Son of Mary,

Jesus, the Son of God;

Jesus, who walked the earth as one of us,

Jesus, who told us the truth,

Jesus, who welcomed us and all with open arms,

Jesus, who healed the sick and blessed the children –

Jesus, who on the night before he died:

took bread, and gave thanks, and broke it

and gave it to his disciples saying:

> "Take and eat, this is my body, given for you.

> Do this in remembrance of me."

After supper, he took the cup, and gave thanks,

and gave it for all to drink, saying,

> "This cup is the new covenant in my blood,

> shed for you and for all people for the forgiveness of

sin.

> Do this in remembrance of me."

Let us proclaim the mystery of faith:

> **Christ has died, Christ is risen, Christ will come
> again.**

O Lord, send your Holy Spirt upon this bread and cup,

making them be for us the body and blood of Christ.

And send your Holy Spirit upon us who gather here,
making us to be the body of Christ for the world.

Amen

Delmer Chilton with John Fairless

FIRST SUNDAY OF ADVENT

Isaiah 64:1-9; Psalm 80:1-7, 17-19; 1 Corinthians 1:3-9; Mark 13:24-37

Notes on the Texts

As you will see in the sermon below, this first Sunday in Advent opens in something of an "apocalyptic" vein. This could be seen as a real challenge – what with our congregations likely ramping up for a holiday mood at home, work, and school – or, we can accept it as an opportunity to embrace the strangeness and break with "business as usual" that is Advent.

It's not supposed to be "business as usual!"

- **Isaiah**'s is an ACTIVE text; God tears the heavens and shakes the mountains. Sinners had best watch out (and, perhaps, straighten up!) But God is also a patient Father, one who does not remember iniquity forever. Whew! (And thank God for that!)

- **Psalm 80** introduces one of Advent's tried and tested themes: light. In particular, the light that shines from the face of God, which is the source of our salvation.

- **1 Corinthians** has us waiting on God's big reveal. It might be fruitful to think of times when you have had to wait on something (like your 16th birthday, or, the birth of a child) with great anticipation. You knew you were eager for the event, but there was also a little anxiety and uncertainty about what the big event might bring.

- **Mark** speaks in those apocalyptic tones we mentioned earlier. Stars falling from the sky, the sun getting dark, the lack of any moon in the sky at night. Again, not exactly the joyous Christmas season that some have come to church expecting! A key thought here might be that it's an especially good time to keep awake – to pay attention and watch what's going on. God might be up to more than we could possibly imagine.

Sermon

As I wrote this, I was sitting in my home study, looking out the window at a driving rain and occasionally checking the Weather Channel for updates on the path of Hurricane Irma.

Here in the Western North Carolina mountains we were far from the devastation in Florida, but there was still enough threat of rain, flood, wind and power outages to cause a bit of anxiety. It was like that for a while. I have dear friends and god-children in Houston and I checked in with them frequently concerning Hurricane Harvey.

I also have close friends in the Seattle area where wildfires were raging. I called one of those friends to check on him and he said he had just driven across the state to Spokane and the smoke and fire were a bit eerie. He mused, "Add this to the hurricanes in the southeast and the nuclear threats from North Korea, and things are feeling a bit 'apocalyptic' these days."

A bit 'apocalyptic' is a good description of our reading from Isaiah and our Gospel lesson:

- **Isaiah 64:1-2** - *O that you would tear open the heavens and come down, so that the mountains would quake at your presence – as when fire kindles brushwood and the fire causes water to boil.*

- **Mk. 13-24-25** - *But in those days, after that suffering, the sun will be darkened, and the moon will not give its light, and the stars will be falling from heaven, and the powers in heaven will be shaken.*

And the question arises – "How are these kinds of Bible lessons supposed to help get us ready for Christmas?" By early December most of us have plans for either traveling to see family or getting the house ready to receive guests. We have school programs, and children's plays, and parties at work or in the community or both. We have presents to buy and wrap, and cards to mail, and meals to prepare, and trips to plan, and, and, and. Again, what does all this "end of times," apocalyptic stuff have to do with 'getting ready for Christmas? Well actually, a lot.

Yogi Berra was reputed to have said, "If you don't know where you're going, you might end up someplace else." Same thing applies in reverse during Advent, "If you don't know what's coming, you might not know it when it gets here."

Most of the world around us is getting ready for a fuzzy and indistinct celebration that is a mishmash of the Biblical Story (summarized by a string of hymn titles: "O Little Town of Bethlehem," "Away in a Manger," "Angels we have heard on High," and "We Three Kings;") plus a bit of English Victorian Sentimentality brought to us by Charles Dickens, topped off with Santa Claus, Rudolph, The Grinch, and "Chestnuts Roasting on an Open Fire." All of which is a lot of fun and very nice, very nice indeed. It just isn't what the Advent season is about. If this mix of sights and sounds and celebrations is all we look for, and get ready for, and prepare for – it is likely to be all that we notice of God coming into the world.

In the 12th century, monastery leader and great preacher Bernard of Clairvaux helpfully stated the overall message of Advent as "The Coming of Christ," and further clarified that in this liturgical season we are:

1) <u>**Remembering**</u> that Christ came **in the flesh** at Bethlehem,

2) <u>**Preparing**</u> for Christ to come daily **in our community** and **in our hearts**

3) <u>**Anticipating**</u> Christ coming again **in the Second Coming.**

Throughout Advent we are invited to remember not only that Christ came in the flesh at Bethlehem, but also why. Our "apocalyptic" texts for today were selected to help us think about why Christ came in the first place and to help us prepare for Christ to come to us again . . . and again, and again.

Isaiah 64 was written by and for a people in exile, people who were living as strangers and aliens in a foreign land. They were a people who had suffered much and had lost everything that defined who they were as the Chosen people of God – their land, their king, their temple. All they had left was the covenant with God summarized in the divine promise that "I will be your God and you shall be my people." (Leviticus 26:12) Isaiah cries out to God, lamenting and confessing the people's sin and reminding God of this promise and imploring God to come and redeem them, rescue them.

The 13th chapter of Mark also alludes to this promise of God to come to God's people. In the many years between the time in the wilderness talked about in Leviticus, the return from exile in Isaiah, and the life of Jesus recorded in Mark; many startling images had been added – sun and moon and stars disturbed, angels flying about, etc., yet the promise remains constant – and the promise remains sure – God will come and God will save.

We are reminded of this history and promise every Sunday. In the middle of the Eucharistic Prayer, we are invited to proclaim the mystery of faith: **Christ has died, Christ is risen, Christ will come again.** We remember not only that Christ was born a baby in Bethlehem, but that he also lived and walked among us, and died upon a cross in Jerusalem. In the words "Christ is risen," we proclaim that the resurrection is not only a past event but also a present reality – Christ living in the world and in our hearts every day. And we look to "that day" when Christ will come again to make all things new.

So, though the world is often quite "apocalyptic," though we be surrounded by wars and rumors of wars, storms and fires both actual and metaphorical, though life may torture us with the remembrance of our faults and failures, our sins and shortcomings – "yet," we can cry out with Isaiah, "O Lord, you are our Father; we are the clay, and you are the potter, we are all the work of your hand;" and we can pray with Paul that "(God) will also strengthen (us) to the end, so that (we) may be blameless on the day of Our Lord Jesus Christ."

Amen and amen.

THE SECOND SUNDAY OF ADVENT

Isaiah 40:1-11; Psalm 85:1-2, 8-13; 2 Peter 3:8-15a; Mark 1:1-8

Notes on the Texts

Ah, comfort! Now there's a holiday-worthy image for a preacher to work with! Thanks, Isaiah!

Only this "comfort" may not be quite what our folks are expecting, either, continuing the theme that Advent may do more to upset our apple cart (if you know what I mean) than help us maintain peace, harmony, and smooth relations with our friends and loved ones.

- **Isaiah** does begin with words of consolation – debts have been paid, sins are being forgiven. But, there is work that remains: the wilderness highway must be prepared. Valleys are to be lifted up – mountains are to be brought low. This is pretty heavy-duty work, when you think about it! Not to mention fading grass and withering flowers. Still, all in all (as John the Baptizer will proclaim,) it's good news in the end. God is a mighty God, with arms that are both strong and tender.

- **Psalm 85** gives an important key for this season of waiting and preparation: "Let me hear what the Lord will speak, for he will speak to peace to his people, to his faithful, to those who turn to him in their hearts." (v.3) This would make a great sermon titled, "Listen, My Children, and You Shall Hear."

- I wouldn't want to get too hung up on the thousand years to a day conversion metrics in **2 Peter**. The real issue is more along the lines of what patience in God's timing looks (and feels) like. Just know this: the wait will be worth it!

- Whatever we learn and experience about Jesus in this high season of worship, remember that it's only the beginning! **Mark** hearkens back to our Isaiah passage (that's a handful, right there!) and connects it to John the Baptizer.

John himself brings a message that connects Jesus to the waters of our baptism and the work of the Holy Spirit in our lives. These are symbols of both the beginning and ongoing nature of God's redemption in our lives and our world.

Sermon

When I was a about 5 or 6 years old I ordered a packet of watermelon seeds; and a packet of pumpkin seeds; and another of cucumbers seeds. The day I got the seeds in the mail I was very excited. Not many weeks later, I was a very disappointed and unhappy young man. It happened like this:

One day in mid-winter I was visiting my grand-parents, which wasn't unusual because they lived next door – well, next-door in farm terms, about a half-mile walk through the woods. Grandpa had just gotten his new seed catalog and I was mesmerized by the pictures of watermelons and pumpkins and cucumbers. I loved cold watermelon and pumpkin pie and sweet, crunchy, cucumber pickles. Grandpa told me that if I could save the money he would order the seeds for me and help me plant them. I think they were 25 cents per package. In 1960 that was a lot of money for a six-year-old with no allowance, but I found it somehow and Grandpa ordered my seeds. When they came in the spring, he helped me prepare a little plot beside his house and showed me how to plant the seeds. I put the empty packets with the alluring pictures of perfect produce on little sticks at the end of the row; for identification, and also as a sign of hope.

And then I waited, and waited, and waited some more. The next morning, I went over to check my garden and there I found, nothing. And the next day? Nothing. And the next? Still nothing. And so it went for a week. Grandpa found me there one morning, tears running down my face. I looked at him and wept, "What did I do wrong?" He picked me up and held me against his chest. I remember hearing his watch ticking in its little pocket in his bib overalls. He laughed a very gentle, caring laugh and said, "Nothing son, nothing at all. It just takes time. Now you have to do the hardest thing anyone ever has to do. You have to wait and trust God."

The season of Advent is about waiting. Waiting for God to act, waiting for God to come. Waiting for seeds of goodness and love to bloom and grow. Waiting, waiting, waiting. And often, in the midst of our waiting, we wonder what we have done wrong.

Amidst all our doubts and worries, our anxious waiting and fear of failure – a voice comes to us. A voice that comforts, comforts God's people, speaks tenderly to us, letting us know that we have done nothing wrong – at least nothing that will keep God from loving us, from forgiving us, from picking us up and holding us, from putting us down and pointing us in the right direction.

John the Baptist is not often thought of as a comforting, tender voice, but he really is. Most of our negative response to John is because of a misunderstanding about the nature of "repentance." Too often, we think of repentance as a sort of "coming clean," of " 'fessing up" to our bad deeds and evil intentions. And often, we not only don't want to do that, we don't see any reason why we should. All this sin and repentance business smacks of either tacky revival preachers pointing fingers and talking about hell; or prissy, puritanical school-teachers standing over us with a ruler in hand, demanding we spit out our gum, or whatever else we enjoy that she disapproves of. And this is, most certainly, not what John the Baptist is talking about.

Repentance is a comforting word, and a part of God's tender mercies for God's beloved people. It reminds us that no failure is forever and that God, unlike most of us, does not hold grudges.

In Hebrew, it's *teshuva,* in Greek it is *metanoia.* Both mean "to turn." This is understood as turning to God and away from evil. Notice the sequence – it is in the act of turning to God that we turn away from evil. Turning to God comes first. We usually get that wrong. We think that God is like us and therefore wants us to feel sorry for being bad; really, really, really, sorry, before forgiving us. That's not true. We are invited to turn to God, and when we do, we have already turned away from the wrong path we had been following. This is the comfort, this is the tender message, of John the Baptist - "return to God, and you will be welcomed with open arms."

There is an interesting line in 2 Peter that confirms the loving and gentle nature of God's forgiveness; and which explains why we must wait, wait, and wait some more for God's kingdom to spring forth into the world. *"The LORD is not slow about his promise, as some think of slowness, but is patient with you, not wanting any to perish, but all to come to repentance."* (3:9)

God waits for us while we wait for God. Sometimes we get in a hurry, often we get impatient.

We grow weary of this world, and we wish God would get on with it, punishing the evil-doers who oppress us and setting things aright in the world. But God waits, waits for all to turn, waits for people to realize that the path they are on is going in the wrong direction. God waits.

And while God waits, God the good shepherd gathers us up into his bosom; and while we wait, we hear the timepiece of eternity gently beating, beating, beating out the rhythm of God's love.

Amen and amen.

THE THIRD SUNDAY OF ADVENT

Isaiah 61:1-4, 8-11; Psalm 126 or Luke 1:46b-55; 1 Thessalonians 5:6-14; John 1:6-8, 19-28

Notes on the Texts

With the texts on this third Sunday of Advent, things begin to feel a little more open, hopeful, even joyful. Which is good, since this is the *Gaudete*, or Sunday of Joy.

- Isaiah paints a picture of what it is like to be oppressed, brokenhearted, held captive and imprisoned. Our parishioners will not need much reminding of life experiences like these – even and especially in the midst of a holiday season, there is plenty of hurt and heartache in their lives. But Isaiah also speaks of joy in the midst of ashes and ruins. There is "fresh" language here: garlands, anointing oil, brides and jewels, shoots and gardens. Wait and watching for the renewal promised by God is a source of joy.

- **Psalm 126** is the "dreamy" psalm – I like it! Dreams are the stuff of our hopes, our best wishes, our life's aspirations. When we dream, we are transported beyond the world of the mundane; for a time, in our dream-like state, it seems that anything is possible. But, this is a dream come true, with the coming of God's promise. There will be some tears along the way – to be sure – but joy is the outcome.

- We're not really sure whether Paul's preaching regularly included a concluding poem or not, but this brief passage from **1 Thessalonians** has eight ready-made points for a good sermon on any occasion! Oh, and remember that all of these actions (rejoice always, give thanks, etc.) are founded on the idea that "the One who calls you is faithful, and he will do this!"

- Evangelist **John** writes about John the Baptizer with several "nots" – not the light, not the Messiah, not Elijah, not "the prophet." JTB tells it plain and simple, just like it is: "I am a voice, crying in the wilderness." On this day, what has God prepared each of us to be and do?

Sermon

The first focus of the so-called "War on Christmas," was the use of public property for religious displays. In thousands of mostly small towns across America, public property had long been used for nativity scenes. In some places in recent years, menorahs have been added to celebrate Hanukah. For many, many years, no one publicly objected to these displays. They seemed to be of a piece with Christmas trees and colored lights on utility poles and other decorations clustered in the business district – a typically American combination of piety and commerce.

But then, people began to sue on the basis of the separation of church and state. No longer was *Freedom OF Religion* enough, some people were demanding *Freedom FROM Religion.* In what became known as the "reindeer clause," the Supreme Court ruled that such displays could continue if they primarily focused on the secular holiday of Christmas by including such non-religious "seasonal" symbols as Frosty the Snow Man, the Grinch, Elves and Santa's workshop, and of course, Rudolph and the rest of the reindeer. One year I found myself staring at such a display with many bright lights, and moving parts, and a huge sign that read "Season's Greetings" in blinking red and green lights. It was simply overwhelming. I looked, and looked, and looked for a Nativity Scene. I finally found one, tucked in beneath a model ski slope.

As I stood there staring at it, a semi-religious friend of mine walked up and said. "It's almost perfect, isn't it?" Startled, I turned to him with my mouth open. He looked at me and grinned,

"I mean, as a bit of garish art it does show where we are – the gentle and warm light of Christ has been overwhelmed and obscured by the garish light of our sentimentality and greed." I started to argue with him, but then I realized I could not; he was most certainly right.

"There was a man sent from God, whose name was John. He came as a witness to the light, so that all might believe through him. He himself was not the light, but he came to testify to the light." (John 1:6-8)

Before pointing fingers at others, it is important for us to realize that all of us can get so caught up in the whirl of "the holiday season," that we forget why we are celebrating, why Christ came, and why that makes us joyful.

We are all capable of allowing the bright lights of advertising and consuming blind our eyes to the light of God's love in Christ. Without care, we too will keep pushing the creche in our hearts aside, tucking it out of the way to make room for more exciting decorations there.

If we are not careful we might forget that the point of having a manger scene is that it awaken in us a sense of wonder at the miracle of the creator of the universe, the Lord God Almighty, becoming a tiny, helpless baby in order to come to us where we are because we are unable to go to where God is.

If we do not watch ourselves carefully, we could ignore the fact that all the gift-buying and gift-giving and gift-getting serve to remind us that God has already given to us the greatest gift of all, the gift of God's self, the gift of the Christ.

We might forget that our annual Christmas dinner is not only a time of family togetherness, it is also a feast of celebration, a festival to celebrate the presence of Emmanuel, "God with-us" in our lives.

We might overlook the reality that the purpose of Christmas lights is not to outshine and obscure the reason for the season, but to point us to the one true light who is coming into the world.

In many services of baptism, a candle is lit and these or similar words are spoken to the newly baptized person, "*Let your light so shine before others that they may see your good works and glorify your Father in heaven.*" (Evangelical Lutheran Worship, p. 231)

John the Baptist is our best example of this. He knew that he himself was not the light. He knew that Jesus was the light. And he knew that he had one simple job - to testify to the light. That is what we are invited to do as well – to show others, in word and deed, the light of Christ.

Amen and amen.

THE FOURTH SUNDAY OF ADVENT

2 Samuel 7:1-11; Luke 1:46-55 or Psalm 89:1-4, 19-26; Romans 16:25-27; Luke 1:26-38

Notes on the Texts

Now that we have arrived at the fourth and final Sunday in Advent, it's safe to get settled in and stay comfortable in our surroundings with the "Christmas story" wrapped warmly all around us. Right?

Not so fast! Our texts open with a jarring message to King David – who had gotten a little too comfortable in his own interpretation of God's message – and close with one of the most disconcerting deliveries ever received from an angel of God.

- **2 Samuel** records the plans of David, after he was settled and comfortable in his house (there's a nice holiday image!) He wanted to do something nice for God, since God had blessed him so well. So, he thought about building a temple. Only, God didn't want a temple – at least not yet! That was God's plan for somebody else. David and Nathan (his usually-dependable household prophet) both get snapped back to reality by a stern message from the Lord. Maybe it's a good time to check our own plans?

- God's steadfast love and faithfulness are great themes in **Psalm 89**. God really is a Rock – a strong foundation upon which to place our faith!

- In **Romans**, God is not only strong – God is also eternally wise. That's a pretty good combination.

- Oh, boy! Luke records the message given to Mary from the angel Gabriel – the foundation of the coming celebration of Christmas. In our minds, it's a sweet and tender story of love, a stable, some gentle animals, and a glorious birth accompanied by choirs of angels. But – in reality, this deliver is pretty shocking to a young (perhaps teen-aged) girl who is busy planning her upcoming wedding. Pregnancy is not generally the normal prelude to walking down the aisle, after all!

But, Mary finds a way to stay calm through it all, and holds on to see the work of God accomplished in God's own way and timing. That's a tough thing for most of us to do! Focus on Mary's prayer: "Her am I, the servant of the Lord; let it be with me according to your word." (v. 38)

Sermon

A few years ago, I saw a little story in Reader's Digest. I clipped it out and filed it under the title: "Perplexed." The writer was a clerk in the admitting office of a hospital.

One very busy day, there was a parade of people coming to her desk. She perfunctorily handed them all clip-boards with pens and admission forms. There was a crowd filling out forms, being interviewed, or being escorted to their rooms. One very timid woman tentatively entered the clerk's office. She handed over her completed admission forms, her insurance card, and her driver's license. Without looking up the clerk took the material and began entering the information into the computer.

Suddenly she asked, "What is your reason for coming to the hospital?" There was such a long pause without an answer that she looked up. The woman was looking at her watch. Finally she said, "Well, I came to visit my sister, but this has taken so long, I'll have to come back tomorrow."

Like I said, I filed it under "perplexed."

Our text says that "Mary was much perplexed . . ." I imagine she was. This was a completely out of the ordinary, startling, bedazzling, confusing, frightening situation. Under the circumstances, perplexed might be a bit of an understatement. First of all, there's an angel in her bedroom. I'm not sure what an angel looks like but, even if an angel just looks like an ordinary human being - waking up to a strange yet ordinary looking someone in your bedroom would be frightening enough.

But there's more, the strange being in her bedroom told her she was going to have a baby. Though Mary is quite young and inexperienced in these matters – she is neither stupid nor ignorant. She knows where babies come from, and she knows she hasn't done that so . . . Huh? What?

Then the angel said that her theoretical baby was going to be the long-awaited messiah, the savior of Israel – and what had been weird became crazy. No wonder Mary was "perplexed."

It is likely that she was also petrified, confused, and scared out of her wits.

It is doubtful that any of us have ever been confronted with an angel in the bedroom, but all of us have found ourselves in perplexing circumstances. We have all been faced with living in a world of uncertain futures, times when our life seems to be out of our hands and out of control. As a Christian people, we stand in the middle of such uncertainties with an added layer of perplexity – we are called of God to be a different sort of folk, a peculiar people the Bible calls us, a royal priesthood, a holy nation. On this last Sunday before Christmas we are reminded that our primary calling is to bring Christ into the midst of our perplexing world.

As we ponder this calling, we can learn from Mary about how to respond to this. We can learn from her humility - the healthy recognition of one's unworthiness. Mary did not immediately assume she deserved the role she was being handed; she did not go about bragging that she had been named #1 in a poll of eligible maidens; she did not "humble brag" about the great honor she had received. Instead, she bowed her head, called herself "a servant of the Lord," and went quietly about the business of trying to explain things to her fiancé.

God has chosen us, the church, to bring Christ into the world. Just as Mary carried the Christ child in her womb so that God could be born into the midst of a needy world – we carry Christ in us, so that God can be born again, and again, and again; in selfless acts of love and sacrifice as we encounter and serve those we meet.

We can also learn from her faith – a quiet, confident trust in God's goodness even in the midst of mysterious and inexplicable goings-on. Mary had no reason to believe that her nocturnal vision was anything other than an odd dream. It was, frankly, no more believable then than it is now; no more reasonable to her than to us. Her outward circumstances did not show that she was carrying within her the inheritor of the "throne of David," the son of God, the Prince of Peace, the king of kings. Just a young girl from a small village, given in marriage to an ordinary working man.

Yet, she held onto the promise, she never let go of the vision, she kept the faith. She held onto that promise, that vision, for almost 35 years. She held onto it through the confusion of his preaching and teaching, his rejection and suffering, his crucifixion and death. And on Easter, she saw the promise fulfilled, the vision realized, the dream become reality.

We too are called this day to hold onto the dream, to believe and remember the promise, to keep the faith, to see God's vision through to the end, to carry Christ into the world with us, no matter how perplexed, or confused, or hesitant we might feel.

Amen and amen.

ADVENT LESSONS AND CAROLS WITH COMMUNION

Suggested for Christmas Eve

GATHERING

Prelude

Gathering Hymn *"Come , Thou Long-expected Jesus"*

Welcome and Worship Notes (*explanation of service*)

Apostolic Greeting and Prayer of the Day

Leader: The Grace of our Lord Jesus Christ,

the love of God,

and the communion of the Holy Spirit be with you all.

People: And also with you.

Leader: Let us pray:

Stir up our hearts, O Holy One,

and prepare us for your advent here - and now.

Open our eyes to see your presence not only in the good that comes

our way,

but also in the evil that cries out for our attention and

response.

Open our arms to reach out not only for your help,

but also in giving aid and assistance to those in needs.

Open our ears to hear not only your words of grace and forgiveness to

us,

but also your call to be graceful and forgiving to our

neighbors.

Stir up our hearts, O Promised One, so that we not only receive love

from you,

but also act in love toward our friends - and our enemies.

All this we pray in the name of Jesus your son and our Lord.

People: AMEN.

PROCLAMATION OF THE WORD

First Reading: Isaiah 40:1-5

Hymn   *"Comfort, Comfort, Now My People"*

Second   Reading Isaiah 40:9-11

Hymn   *"Come   , Thou Long-expected Jesus"*

Third Reading   Isaiah 60:1-3, 19-20

Hymn   *"O Come, O Come, Emmanuel!"*

Fourth   Reading Zephaniah 3:14-20

Hymn   *"Hark, the Glad Sound"*

Fifth Reading   Psalm 89:1-4, 19-26

Hymn   *"How Long, O Lord"*

Sixth Reading   Luke 1:26-38

Hymn   *"Savior of the Nations, Come"*

Seventh   Reading Luke 1: 46-55

Choir Anthem or Solo Rendition of *"The Magnificat"*

Homily

OUR RESPONSE TO GOD'S WORD

Creed *(for those who use Creeds)*

I believe in God, the Father almighty,
    creator of heaven and earth;

I believe in Jesus Christ, his only Son, our Lord.
    He was conceived by the power of the Holy Spirit
        and born of the Virgin Mary.
    He suffered under Pontius Pilate,
        was crucified, died, and was buried.
    He descended to the dead.
    On the third day he rose again.
    He ascended into heaven,
        and is seated at the right hand of the Father.
    He will come again to judge the living and the dead.

I believe in the Holy Spirit,
    the holy catholic Church,
    the communion of saints,
    the forgiveness of sins
    the resurrection of the body,
    and the life everlasting. Amen.

Biblical Statement of Faith *(for those who don't)*

Minister: Christ Jesus, who, though he was in the form of God,

            did not regard equality with God as something to be
exploited,

People: But emptied himself, taking on the form of a slave,

            being born in human likeness.

Minister: And being found in human form, he humbled himself

            and became obedient to the point of death – even death on a
cross.

People: Therefore, God also highly exalted him

and gave him the name that is above every name,

Minister: So that at the name of Jesus, every knee should bend,

in heaven and on earth and under the earth,

People: And every tongue should confess that Jesus Christ is Lord! AMEN.

(Philippians 2:5b-11a; NRSV)

Prayers of the People

Leader: Let us pray for our world, our community, our church, and ourselves.

Leader: *O Come, O Come, Emmanuel;* your whole creation aches, and groans, and yearns,

for your advent among us. Come to us and lead us as we work to heal our land, our water, and our air. Come into our midst and show us the way to remove the walls that separate us, to mend the disagreements that have ruptured the peace and justice you mean for us to have. *O Come, O Come, Emmanuel,*

People: **And ransom captive Israel.**

Leader: *Savior of the nations, come;* come and teach the leaders of the world, the leaders of our nation, the leaders of our state, the leaders of our community, how to be peace-makers. Savior of the nations, come and teach each of us how to work for peace in a world full of conflict and war; stir us up to labor for justice in a world struggling with unfairness and unbridled ambition. Savior of the nations, come, and help us understand what your mother Mary knew – that you did not come to make our life better – you came to change the life of the world for the better through us. *Savior of the nations, come,*

People: **Virgin's Son, make our hearts your home.**

Leader: *How long, O Lord,* will your church sit in darkness, yearning to see the light? How long must we wait until the Kingdom comes in full? How long before we see the world becoming the place of peace and love that we believe in, that we work toward, that we were promised?

Be with us Lord, and teach us to wait patiently for your full kingdom, while impatiently living by kingdom standards now. Help us be the holy community you created us to be, the body of Christ in the world that can say with joyful and expectant hearts, *How long, O Lord?*

People: Not Long! Come Lord Jesus!

Leader: *Comfort, comfort now your people.* O God of love and comfort, your church awaits your coming with joy and hope. There are many among us who are suffering. Some feel despair, some are tired from sickness, others are weary from tending to the sick. Many remember with sadness the friends and family who have died and are no longer here. Some are anxious about their children, other worry about their parents, we all fret about ourselves. *Comfort, comfort now your people* Lord, especially (*names . . .*), that they may find healing and hold onto the promise that:

People: You, O lord our God, will reign in peace forever.

Leader: We release all these worries into your hands, trusting fully in your never-ending grace and your faithful promise to come again. **AMEN.**

Peace

THE COMMUNION

Offering and   **Offertory**   *"What Child is this?"*
(Hymn is sung as the plates are passed and the table is prepared.
Congregation stands and sings verse three - "So bring him incense, gold . . ."
as offering is presented at the table.)

Dialog

> **Minister:** The Lord be with you.
>
> **People: And also with you.**
>
> **Minister:** Lift up your hearts.
>
> **People: We lift them up to the Lord.**
>
> **Minister:** Let us give thanks to the Lord our God.
>
> **People: It is right to give God our thanks and praise.**

Preface

> **Minister:** It is a good and joyful thing that we should,
>
>   at all times and in all places,
>
>   give thanks and praise to you, O God,
>
>   our creator and sustainer.
>
>   Through prophets and preachers,
>
>   patriarchs and matriarchs,
>
>   women and men judges,
>
>   kings and queens,
>
>   those in high places
>
>   and those who simply tilled the soil and tended the sheep
>
>   - you have reached out to us in word and deed
>
>   to teach, guide, rebuke and inspire us.

And then you sent to us the greatest gift of all,

the gift of yourself

in the person of your Son,

Jesus Christ our Lord.

And so, with Gabriel and Mary.

with all the saints above

and all the sinners below,

we unite our voices in heaven's eternal song

of thanksgiving and praise:

Holy, Holy, Holy, Lord,

God of power and might.

Heaven and earth are full of your glory.

Hosanna in the highest.

Blessed is the one who comes in the name of the Lord.

Hosanna in the highest.

Communion Prayer

Blessed are you,

O Lord of the universe and Lord of our hearts,

we praise you for

your power and your tenderness;

your justice and your mercy,

your demand that we be righteous

and your command that we love one another.

On this day,

we have recalled in word and song

the many times
you have rescued your people from themselves
and have promised to lift us up and revive us, again.

On this day,
we celebrate the fulfillment of those promises
in Jesus of Nazareth,
Jesus, the Son of Mary,
Jesus, the Son of God;
Jesus, who walked the earth as one of us,
Jesus, who told us the truth,
Jesus, who welcomed us and all with open arms,
Jesus, who healed the sick and blessed the children –

Jesus, who on the night before he died:
took bread, and gave thanks, and broke it
and gave it to his disciples saying:
"Take and eat, this is my body, given for you.
Do this in remembrance of me."

After supper, he took the cup, and gave thanks,
and gave it for all to drink, saying,
"This cup is the new covenant in my blood,
shed for you and for all people for the forgiveness of
sin.
Do this in remembrance of me."

Let us proclaim the mystery of faith:

Christ has died, Christ is risen, Christ will come again.

O Lord, send your Holy Spirt upon this bread and cup, making them be for us the body and blood of Christ.

And send your Holy Spirit upon us who gather here, making us to be the body of Christ for the world.

Amen

Minister: With the boldness and joy of beloved children of God, let us pray

The Lord's Prayer:

Our Father in heaven, hallowed be your Name, your kingdom come, your will be done, on earth as in heaven.
Give us today our daily bread.
Forgive us our sins, as we forgive those who sin against us.
Save us from the time of trial, and deliver us from evil.
For the kingdom, the power, and the glory are yours, now and forever.
Amen.

The Breaking of the Bread and the Invitation to the Table

Minister: Come ye that seek the Lord, the Table is now prepared.

These are the gifts of God for the very much beloved people of God.

People: Thanks be to God.

Congregational hymns to be sung during communion:

O Come, All Ye Faithful
Angels We Have Heard on High
Away in a Manger

SENDING INTO THE WORLD

Prayer After Communion

Minister: Let us pray.

People: Thank you, O Lord, that you have fed us with this gift of life and love. Send us forth from this table to share this same life and love

with all those whom we meet each day. AMEN.

Blessing

Minister: May the God who keeps promises;

the Creator who made us,

the Son who saved us,

and the Holy Spirit who propels us on our way,

be with you all, now and forever more.

Amen

Sending   Hymn   *"Joy to the World"*

Dismissal

Leader: Go in peace. Spread the Good News.

People: Thanks be to God

Postlude

About the Authors

Delmer Chilton and John Fairless have been friends, colleagues, and collaborators on scriptural and church-type projects for more than 20 years.

They are the co-creators of **The Lectionary Lab** website and podcast, co-authors of *The Lectionary Lab Commentary Series* (Volumes for Years A, B, and C,) and *A Simple Way to Preach*, a book that says as much about themselves as it does their homiletical method.

All works are available on Amazon.com.

A HANDFUL OF ADVENT

Made in the USA
Middletown, DE
11 December 2017